Soul Mates

Soul Mates

Agape Love Poems

By Cedric Mixon

Kobalt Books
Saint Louis, MO

SOUL MATES: AGAPE LOVE POEMS

© 2004 by Cedric Mixon

ISBN: 0-9754357-9-5

Cover design by Holly Lane at Zebra Lane L.L.C.
Illustrations by Holly Lane at Zebra Lane L.L.C.

Scripture quotations are from:
The Holy Bible, New King James Version
© 1984 Thomas Nelson, Inc.

For information:
Kobalt Books L.L.C.
P.O. Box 771912,
Saint Louis, MO 63177
Printed in the U.S.A
www.kobaltbooks.com

Soul Mates Introduction 7

Agape Love 8

What You Did That Day 10

Beauty Viewed From Night 11

Distance 13

Love 15

Speechless 16

By My Side 17

So Long...Just Hoping 18

The Possibility 20

Waiting 21

A Companion 22

The Rose 23

Our Love 24

Windows 25

My Butterfly 26

Inside Me 28

Always Love You 29

The Separation 31

Yet Another 32

Thoughts Of Love 33

The Most Beautiful 34

If You Love Someone, It Shows 35

Just Love Me 36

Without A Word 37

If I... 38

Behold The Queen 39

I Feel Loved 40

You Are Love 41

Your Song 42

Love And Water 44

The Search 46

Unbelievable 47

Too Much 48

Asleep 49

Falling 50

The Value Of Your Love 51

Your Voice 52

In Need 53

Tension 54

The Message 55

That's My Song 57

Soul Mates Introduction

"Let me stare deeply into the eyes of the one who comes from me…"

- Cedric Mixon

Then the rib which the Lord God had taken from man He made into a woman, and He brought her to the man.
Genesis 2:22 [NKJV]

Agape Love

You are Love,
First name Agape.
Most don't call You that...

My desire is to know You.

The way
You love imperfect buildings
Where children gather
In Your name...
Just to feel Your presence.
And me...
I reside miles from perfection.

To see with my heart,
And love the same,
Give me vision like blind.
Like minds
Possess similar motives,
Standing close to
You to learn
Seemingly simple principles.
Agape...Unconditional...Love...
Shoulders that bear
World's weight,
And never breaks.

Your sweet voice
Soothes my soul
As 23rd Psalm.
That's my song...

Angelic melodies dance
On ear drums,
And I move

To their rhythm.

Mind-state as Mercury
Who dances closest to Your Son (Sun),
With other stars,
And planets,
Who also tap their
Feet to the beat.

Your life-poetry's
The lyrics.
Former heart that aches...
Pain redirected
To muscles in face,
That responds to laughter
In my spirit.

You speak through the gentle
Breeze that tickles my
Facial hair follicles,
And forms joy-tears,
That washes away
Misery molecules.

What You Did That Day

The day
You looked into my eyes,
And saw my soul.
Touched my chest
And reached into my heart.
Wrote poetry
On it.
Love songs
With the strongest
Feeling.
Mind elevated,
And You launched it.
You held my hand
And my life together.
My umbrella
In stormy weather.
You walk a straight line.
Take my
Hand
And...Bring me with You.
Sang to my ears,
Heart, and soul
With one melody...
Voice so heavenly.

Kissed my cheek,
And melted hard exterior.

Loved me unconditionally,
And showed me
What it means.

Beauty Viewed From Night

Warm inside
As location
Where heart beats.
To which You speak...
But I listen with ears.
So it's not me,
You desire.

Could it be?

Born blind...
Eyes have not seen
Such beauty.

Do You know me?
Felt not Your hands,
But Your Words hold me.

The night...
My only companion
Before I met You.

Shine bright
Like the illumination
Of the moon
That contrasts
Midnight.

And me...
I sit in dark corners
Staring at the
Glow

Of Your soul.

Joy tears drip
From eyes
And quench thirst
Of the meek.

Submerged in a sea
Of mercy.
You forgive
The undeserving.

Life's maestro…
Hand me the cello.
People
Confuse it with
The night's Bistro...
These medley's
Heavenly.

Angels accompany
This solo
And make symphony.

All for You...
The only light
In my life.

Distance

Separated by distance
That adds to itself
As time.
Propelling my mental
To unknown dimensions.
Imposing friendly conversation
As words
Run together
As children.

Eyes like North Star
That I gaze into.
New found direction...
The tension
Of the distance,
That stretches
East and West.

You speak
With beautiful voice
Heard from mockingbird.

The atmosphere
Between us...
More like concrete.
Yet You have no problem
Penetrating the source
Of my heart beat.

My reality...
Losing grip...
Hanging on every word

From Your lips.

My heart roams
Where You desire...
Hypnotized by
Your sweet aroma.

Frustrated with
The line that divides
You and I.

Love

Undeserving of You
As life itself.
You exist
Within the inner
Crevasses of me.

The way you feel...
The way you mold lives.
Making change and...
Too much sense.

Bright like sunrays
That touches hearts
And melts mine to Yours.
Stained in my brain
Forever all because...

It's You...
Your smile...
Your Love.

Speechless

Mental pictures
That don't translate
To ears language.
Overtaken
With cold-weather frustration
That quivers the body.
Releasing,
Leaving behind an empty shell...
Like one-shot
To expose my soul.
No clothes,
I walk spiritually naked,
Until I circle the globe.
Seeking love
That left my heart
To return as the blood
That pumps
Through
Arteries, and...
I'll die without
Your movement
On my inner.
Leaving me
Cold as winter ice
That never melts,
No matter the weather.
I suffer from voice
With no projection...
That freezes in mid-air,
To crash to the ground,
Shatter, and...
I just want to talk to You.

By My Side

By my side...
Walking with me...
Sitting with me...
Just your company is enough.

No matter what they say,
I know how I feel.
I know what You've done.
I remember.

Being average
Blends with "nothing".
Your miraculous ways
So great
Evidence viewed
By universe,
For thoughs
Who desire sight.

So Long...Just Hoping

Elegant perfection
In my dreams...
I...Know you like that.
Authenticity makes me write that.

Pen to paper
Scribbling poems
That makes homes,
And place minds
Where hearts roam.

Can't take this.
Separated by more Miles
Than Davis.

Lucky
I don't play the...trumpet.

Instead, I play this
Song
With pen and paper
Alone.

Write to my heart.
Cause mind gone
Like time is.
Affection forgotten,
But your words
Remind him.

Wondering what
You speak of.
What people

Soul Mates: Agape Love Poems

Have You embraced?

Thoughts suggest jealousy.
Knowing You touched hearts of
Someone else but me.

You talk not to me,
Or perhaps I stopped listening.
Never looked into
The glistening
Of Your eyes.
Therefore truth missed,
All while,
Thinking it was I.

Years since
Heavenly sounds broke
Through clogged ears.
Your voice heard
In words never spoken.
It's been So Long...
Just hoping...

I want You near...
I need You...
Just hoping You feel the same.

The Possibility

Delivered from
Prison-vision
That traps physical.

The Possibility...
Hope...
Free as imagination
That dreams
Past skies
That cloud present.

Reaching for infinity,
With short arms
And open hands.

Just the touch...

All creation's greatness,
Yet You dwell
Within my heart.
Inner drums
Quicken
To a new beat...
And I dance.
I run...
Feet compete
With each other, and…

I smile at The Possibility...

Waiting

Calling and...Calling...
Wondering Your location.

Lonely...Vulnerable...

Love unrequited
It seems yet again.

Familiar feeling…

Wind whispers
To eager ears.

"Maybe you're not ready..."
"I am preparing you..."

"And me...I'm just waiting."

A Companion

My chest contracts,
While I nap,
And I dream of words that,
Bring to existence,
One who's yoke is similar.
The labor of the land,
Is the fruit of Your hands.
My chest expands.

Worth more than diamonds,
Rubies and pearls.
I carry the world's weight,
On my shoulders for the reason,
Of granting a strong place for You to lean on.
Your brush creates the depiction.
But words and verbs,
Disperse from the soul,
To paint this picture.

Have You seen my rib?
Missing one as I awaken,
Waiting for the day when,
The Divine Master-Piece is finished.
Until then...
Lonely I sit admiring the mansion,
For us to share when,
My prayer is...
Lord, please grant a,
Friend that,
Understands my,
Love for You.

A Companion...

The Rose

Sleep, I am,
Dreaming of you…
Trying not to wake.
Crying, I pray,
For our embrace.
Envisioning visiting,
Your inner-spirit when,
Living consists of,
Separate existences.
You…Made for I,
I say that I,
Wait for the day that Christ,
Blesses me.
Who less than me,
Satisfies your questioning?
I'll rest in peace,
Knowing that you sleep the same,
I am your Novocain,
To decrease the pain.
Red…Pink…
At times even yellow pedals,
Melt hearts better,
Than summer weather.
You stand near no one else alone,
Like singing acapello.

Where I once would go,
I go no more.
I stop to smell The Rose,
With eyes closed…
Your neck to my nose,
I witness your growth…
God bless The Rose…

Our Love

Oh… What to say,
To make you stay?
Attempting to display,
What you mean to me.
Praying that you never go away,
And the same for Our Love.

I read between the lines,
Of the look in your eyes,
As our souls intertwine.
Hoping you find time,
To read mine,
And these words find,
Your heart, and make you smile.

I need you, like I need to breathe…
Like I need to see…
Secondly,
To my need,
For the Almighty…
I'm likely to never sleep,
If you were separated from me.

The 'Unquestionable',
Is the only One,
That can separate us,
Due to the death of us.
Feeling a slight quiver in my bones,
With just the thought of ever being alone,
After being shown,
The debts of true love.
Our love…
A gift from above.

Windows

Eyes closed…
Horizontal you lay.
Tears reach nose,
And soak clothes.

Deep stares,
Penetrate,
Skin,
And visits within.

Spiritual kiss,
That resembles,
Experiences,
Of physical.
Embracing your innocence.
Security symbol…
Gazing through infinite,
Levels of windows.
Simple…Love.

The calmness that comes from gazing through the window is a moment of love. This is a moment when fond memories are recalled. Through the window, I watch love come and go, and I remember.

My Butterfly

Spiritually abused…
Cocoon bruises,
Form muse.

Strong wings flutter.
Who other,
Than My Butterfly.

Asleep waiting,
Your arrival.
Pushing through,
Current situations,
Placing you,
In my arms embracing.
Wings elevate you,
To heights,
Greater than,
Scenes from,
Pinnacles of skyscrapers.

"You elevate my mind,
Propelling my spirit beyond the moon...
Conversing with stars
That illuminate universal darkness..."
-Cedric Mixon

Inside Me

It's inside of me.
Tribulations covered
In flashy exterior.

Running and running...
Can't escape me.
It's with whom I live.

Work on me...
Things the world
Notices not.

Love me...
Move inside me...
To my heart.

Always Love You

The allure of
Love more pure than
Water that drips
From mountain tops,
And quenches thirst,
As fountain drops.

To ears
I create music
Which reassures I...
Will always love You.

Indescribable spirit which
Transcends physical.
Souls unified
As two worlds collide,
Giving birth to love...
First name agape.
Your love traces
Straight and narrow,
And I follow
With perfect posture.

The way You laugh,
Move, heal,
And worship...
So perfect.
Transform worthless
Life to purpose.

Voice projects an
Expression
Equivalent to heavenly

Soul Mates: Agape Love Poems

Symphony.
More than attraction,
Its divine chemistry.

The love I speak,
Precedes
Adam and Eve,
And romance...
Instead I hold hands
With Omnipotence.
And...I will always love you.

The Separation

My love for life,
Was dependant on your breathing.
Once your breath ended,
I had no reason,
For living.

Closed eyes,
Watch you walk out my life,
Seeing pain, as the blind,
And remembering times,
Of happiness.
My heart aches,
As I partake,
Sadness deeply within my abdomen.
Why do I feel abandoned?

Empty in the,
Physical and the spiritual.
I know the Lord listens to,
My almost sinful opinions.

From this...Blessings will come,
So let Your Will be done.
I see nothing,
But continue running,
Until I pass my troubles.
Merely feeling the frustrations,
Of The Separation.

Yet Another

God heads life.
Shared soul,
As friend…
As wife…

Lift spirits,
To heights,
Of greater flight.

Joy tears flow,
To tip of nose.
Former froze soul,
Experiences relief,
From cold.

Thoughts Of Love

Thoughts of Love...
The moment we first touched...
Our first kiss,
Simple yet,
Seemed more intimate.

For a chest that's hurting,
You resemble a surgeon,
To handle a heart that's aching,
From past situations.

Our togetherness,
Resembles the mere sentiment,
Of Heaven.
Placing my mental residence,
Far from any place of remembrance.

Live without you...
I pray this day,
Never takes place,
Or for sure I'll live lost...
My life "the maze."
Words as poetry,
For you...For me...
Even if I speak,
To closed walls,
And the only,
One who hears me,
Is The Almighty.

Screaming my love for you,
Hearing nothing but the reflected echo,
Symbolizing solitude.

The Most Beautiful

You Smile,
While sunshine,
Fills the room.
More love than birth,
From a mother's womb.

The Most Beautiful...

Eternal Youthful days,
As I gaze,
Into your eyes.
Rendering,
Another reason,
For life.

Your essence,
Presses against the center,
Of my heart.
Yet leaves no evidence,
Of chest pains.
Your warmth dries tears,
Before my face is stained.

My heart sings,
As the mockingbird.
Melodies intervene,
With the Heavenly breeze,
Placing my Spirit,
On High as the wind,
Under eagle's wings.

The Most Beautiful in the World.

If You Love Someone, It Shows

If You Love Someone, It Shows,
Love grows,
More than the one who stands on his toes.

The Sweet smell of,
One pedal,
Of a rose.
Won't allow me to let go,
Of the affect of,
Your Love.

Stare deeply through my eyes,
Not to where I have sight,
But to where I cry.
Shy away from the trials,
Or anything that leaves me asking why.

Lying at the bottom of the sea,
I can still breathe,
And I know You Love me.
Though on the surface it seems,
I've been abandoned with no hope,
And no rope,
To climb to where I can inhale fresh air though my nose.
But instead of drowning, I float,
And quickly reflect from where my thoughts flow.
If You Love Someone, It Shows.

Just Love Me

As I am,
Love me for me.

Can't endure
My own existence...
Love me, for me.

Fortunate fate
Misplaced...
Everything lost,
I survive on
Your Love
To map-me
Through maze.

Shine bright
Like fog lights,
For cloudy tomorrows
That overwhelms vision.

When other offers
Outweigh
My love's mass,
Stand with me...
Love enough
For the both of us.

Without A Word

Could it be the brown skin,
That brings me as high as the mountain,
When before, I was drowning?

Who possesses a smile so lovely,
That places my life above the,
View that the doves see?

Staring at you,
With what's heard,
Is not the chirp of a bird,
Or a kitten's purr,
But, the sound of two souls that merge,
With the connection of the ribs first,
And the passing of leaves, in the breeze,
Without a Word.

If I...

If I cause pain,
To stain your heart,
Then I accept the blame,
And acknowledge the shame,
All the same.

If I lack better judgment,
Then I accept the punishment,
For hurting you.

Divine Wisdom speaks clearly...
"Be careful how you treat your gift..."
My dearly
Beloved,
Placed near me,
To hear the,
Solitary weeping...
To heal these,
Lonely evenings.

If I ponder perfection,
When I dream,
Forgive me...
So innocent... You seem,
To resemble these scenes,
In my mind.
Your skin... Your eyes...
Your smile...
I love You...

Behold The Queen

Noticing beauty…

I place my eyes,
On what lies,
Across the room as I,
Sit and admire.

A heart more peaceful,
Than God's Chosen People.

A Spiritual Being,
Plus a vibrant thing.

Hold me,
Close or cling,
To my heart,
That you stole…Please
Don't cry from the,
Trials of greater size of the,
Ocean deep.
Just hold me,
As we walk the road that
Leads to Your hopes and dreams.

I fold one knee,
Kissing Your palm,
Expressing vocally...
Behold The Queen.

I Feel Loved

To You,
I stand close.
Smelling scents
That soothes soul.

Your breathe
Breezes past ears
As soft whispers,
And I listen.

Feel wanted...
Feel needed...

I belong.
Looking beyond
Clouds to
Heaven so blue.
I Feel Loved, and...
I know that You do.

You Are Love

You are calm
When waves soak feet
That walk on water.

Your palm catches
Tears that flow
Down cheek
When expected to
Hit rock bottom.

Love is what You do...
Love is who You are.

Your Song

Perfect harmony
For Your song
You sing...
Love You bring,
Gentle touch
For strings.

With that perfection
You bless in
Less than
A second.

Cut through hearts
With precision
To get in.

And leave no heart aches.
Instead I part ways
With dark days.

Replaced with
Amazing Graces.
Notes played in
Minds until the day when
You change songs.
Hear that?
Ears ain't wrong.

Multiple octaves
With
Complex chords.
Unpredictable melody
From voice

Soul Mates: Agape Love Poems

Of My Lord.

Jazz...Gospel...
Not quite rhyme.
More than classical,
Your Song divine.

Blesses in
Abundance.
Calm breeze
For wind instruments
That destroys walls
Of Jericho...
And I the trumpet.

Best gift ever
For two lips.
It's Your Song,
Use me
To create music.

Love And Water

Your Love…
Like water
That washes the sand from my feet.
When it should be me
Who washes yours.
So hot
Your Love
Exudes from pores.

Your Love
As nourishment recycled…
Touching every
Soul on the globe
While providing
Cleansing.
And I, the
Fish that swims
In Your heart open,
While Your Love
Touches all lands,
As waves of ocean.

Your love
Freely flows from
Crying clouds
And blossoms blessings.

Thirsty with
Dry throat
Made moist
To rejoice.
Just the drip sound
Of one drop

Soul Mates: Agape Love Poems

Gives hope enough.

Love more pure than
Water formed in spring.
Your Love brings
Life to the lifeless.
Motion to the stagnant.
Clear as Your existence.

Hot or cold,
Water is still wet.
No matter the
Temperature degrees,
You keep the same properties
From above.
You are Love.

The Search

In search
Of someone
I know not of.
However...
I am certain
Of what I'm looking for.
One who resembles
Me in the spiritual
Opposite my physical.
The most beautiful...
I compliment her.

Unbelievable

Attempting to understand
Your love.
Created from dust
To worship.

Lump in throat...
So hard to swallow
The possibility of
You just wanting a friend.
Hard to grasp,
As the concept
Slides through
My mind.

And all You ask
For is love returned.

The seemingly small things You do
Make big blessings
Seem unbelievable.
Forgive me,
For not believing.

Too Much

So amazing...
Far above my mental realm.
Words play in my mind,
And run together.

Circle the notion
Of Your unconditional love.

Your universal existence
Alone
Overwhelms me.

Asleep

Eyes closed,
Envisioning your creation.
Born again...
Actually birthed years ago.

Dreaming...
I ask your name,
With no reply.
Where are you from?

You reply,
God's heart and vision,
Without moving your lips.
Asleep while you're
cleverly constructed.
Painted and sculpted
By the greatest artist.

Wanting to awake
And add input...
Embrace the
Creation...
Behold the masterpiece.
But eyes squeezed tight.
Alas...You are not ready.
And apparently,
I am not either.

So I sleep.
I prepare.
I position.

Anxious to talk to you...again.

Falling

Stuck without Your love...

My desires
Seem higher
Than anything asked for,
Or expected.
Looking forward.
But slide backwards,
No matter the elevation
Of my mind.
I fall to knees...
The only place to go.

The Value Of Your Love

Love more valuable
Than any subject
Of mental thoughts.

Nothing exists of comparison.

No one paid more...
For me.

Can't put a figure to Your
Goodness and mercy.
Praise turns to worship.
Not just for what You've done,
Thank You for being You.

Your Voice

The Heavens speak
Of God's Glory.
The rain converses
With the wind...
All nature knows
His story.

God's eye
On the fallen sparrow.
The lily dressed
In fine clothing.
Your Voice heard
From highest mountain,
To valley's lowest.

In Need

No matter how dark...
You are there.

Won't let go
Until You bless my soul.

You move on empty.
Fond of my needs,
To fulfill.
And...I am In Need...
In Need of Your Love.
Bless me
With Your presence.

Tension

Next to you,
I sit.
Wishing to subtract
From this
Three feet of separation.

The invisible line
That only lovers cross.
Hoping the transparency
And poor vision
Are excuse enough.
Where does that leave us?

Avoiding the look of Your eyes.
Knowing You'll
See thoughts as psychic.
Secret desires
Exposed when writing.
Love behind the wheel
That drives me crazy.

The Message

A relevant message
With conviction,
Trapped in my
Mental prison.

Seeking true freedom
To express what God says.
Release me...
Loosen the grip
That holds me to my past...
Imprisoned by yesterday
To serve eternal sentence
With no periods
Of meditative worship.
Mouth open with words
Who never discover their purpose,
To make sound waves
That greet ears.
Fear of failure,
And failures biggest fear,
Is not having someone to control.

Thoughts crowd my brain cavity,
Never to be set free.
A clear message of confusion,
That costs nothing, and everything
At the same time.

Temperature rises,
Pressure increases
To force an explosion.
Explode like C-4...
To see for a lost generation,

And bless them with the same vision,
As the reflection from mirrors.

Grant the desire to elevate minds
Higher than any illegal substance.
The message bares substance
For your soul.
His love warm
When your heart, cold.

Equal opposites that attract
As the positive proton
Of this electronic world.
The message is not I...
Yet moves within as blood
Warm in veins.
Flowing through each of us...
Same message, different voice.

That's My Song

What should I sing about?

Smiles that stretch miles?
Sunshine that gives sight
To eyes that focus
On Your Sun (Son),
And blesses the blind
Who never saw Your love
Through the darkness
The camouflages the pain.

Mercy for this unworthy...
Life to this life...
Soul saved
With no account for
Sinful riches.
Completeness
When feeling lonely...

I won't complain at all...
That's My Song.

Evaporation
When rain pours
And soaks clothes...
When tears
Drip from tip
Of nose.
They never hit the ground.

"Mind-state as Mercury
Who dances closest to Your Son (Sun),
With other stars,
And planets,
Who also tap their
Feet to the beat..."

- Cedric Mixon

Coming January, 2006
Survival Poetry Series, Book Four

Can You Love Me?

Survival Poetry Series, Book Two
"Boldly Walking Naked: Short Poems for Daily Survival"
ISBN: 0-9754357-3-6
Available Now…

Survival Poetry Series, Book One
"Lost Letters: Short Poems for Spiritual Resurrection"
ISBN: 0-9754357-7-9
Available Now…

www.kobaltbooks.com

Cover Art and Design by

ZEBRA LANE

www.zebralane.com

www.ingramcontent.com/pod-product-compliance
Lightning Source LLC
Chambersburg PA
CBHW031333040426
42443CB00005B/323